# Giggle Fit™

# School Jokes

Joseph Rosenbloom

Illustrated by
Steve Harpster

Sterling Publishing Co., Inc.
New York

**Library of Congress Cataloging-in-Publication Data Available**

10   9   8   7   6   5   4   3   2   1

Published by Sterling Publishing Co., Inc.
387 Park Avenue South, New York, N.Y. 10016
© 2003 by Sterling Publishing
Distributed in Canada by Sterling Publishing
$c/o$ Canadian Manda Group, One Atlantic Avenue, Suite 105
Toronto, Ontario, Canada M6K 3E7
Distributed in Great Britain by Chris Lloyd at Orca
Book Services, Stanley House, Fleets Lane, Poole BH15 3AJ, England
Distributed in Australia by Capricorn Link (Australia) Pty. Ltd.
P.O. Box 704, Windsor, NSW 2756 Australia

Sterling  ISBN 1-4027-0440-2

What is the first thing a little vampire learns in school?

**The alpha-bat.**

What do little astronauts get when they do their homework?

**Gold stars.**

What do little elves do after school?

**Gnomework.**

What is the first thing a little gorilla learns in school?

**His Ape B C's.**

Where do little monsters study?
**At ghoul school.**

Where did King Arthur study?
**In knight school.**

Where do you go to learn how
to make ice cream?
**Sundae school.**

At what school do you have to drop out in order to graduate?
**Parachute school.**

Why did the one-eyed monster close down his school?
**He only had one pupil.**

What school has a sign on it that says "Please don't knock"?
**Karate school.**

**TEACHER:** How did you find school today?

**PATTY:** Oh, I just got off the bus — and there it was!

Why are school buses yellow?
**They ran out of purple.**

What is yellow outside, gray inside and very crowded?
**A school bus full of elephants.**

Why did the little snake have to stay after school?
**Because it hissed the bus.**

What is the difference between a school bus driver and a cold?
**One knows the stops and the other stops the nose.**

What would happen if you took the school bus home?
**The police would make you bring it back.**

Why did the two-headed monster get good grades?

**Two heads are better than one.**

Why did the firefly get good grades?

**It was very bright.**

Why did the elephant get good grades?

**It had a lot of gray matter.**

Why did the werewolf get good grades?

**He gave snappy answers.**

Why did the balloon get good grades?
**It went to the top of the class.**

Why did the owl flunk out?
**It didn't give a hoot.**

Why did the duck flunk out?
**He was a wise quacker.**

Why did the little skeleton flunk out?
**His heart wasn't in it.**

**SUZY:**  Teacher, may I leave the room?

**TEACHER:**  Well, you certainly can't take it with you.

**TEACHER:**  Barney, you aren't paying attention. Are you having trouble hearing?

**BARNEY:**  No, teacher, I'm having trouble listening.

**TEACHER:**  When you yawn, you're supposed to put your hand to your mouth.

**HARVEY:**  What? And get bitten?

**TEACHER:**  That's quite a cough you have, Mitzi. What are you taking for it?

**MITZI:**  I don't know, teacher. What will you give me?

**TEACHER:** How old were you on your last birthday?

**CHRISSIE:** Seven.

**TEACHER:** How old will you be on your next birthday?

**CHRISSIE:** Nine.

**TEACHER:** That's impossible.

**CHRISSIE:** No, it isn't, Teacher. I'm eight today.

**TEACHER:** Freddie, are you the youngest member of your family?

**FREDDIE:** No, my puppy is.

**TEACHER:** Eddie, name one important thing we have today that we didn't have ten years ago.

**EDDIE:** Me!

### I don't have my homework because

my little sister ate it.

I lent it to a friend, but he moved away.

our furnace broke down and we had to burn it to keep from freezing.

a sudden gust of wind blew it out of my hands and I never saw it again.

a kid fell in the lake and I jumped in to rescue him. But my homework drowned.

**TEACHER:** This homework looks like your father's writing.

**DWIGHT:** Sure, I used his pen.

**DONNA:** Teacher, would you punish me for something I didn't do?

**TEACHER:** Of course not.

**DONNA:** Well, I didn't do my homework.

**TOMMY:** Dad, could you help me with my homework?

**DAD:** No, it wouldn't be right.

**TOMMY:** Well, would you at least give it a try?

**FATHER:** When Lincoln was your age, he did all his homework by candlelight.

**JUNIOR:** And when he was your age, he was president.

**FATHER:** When I was your age, I thought nothing of walking ten miles to school.

**JUNIOR:** I agree, Dad. I don't think much of it either.

**TEACHER:** Why are you late?

**AMOS:** I couldn't find my homework.

**TEACHER:** And why are you late, Oliver?

**OLIVER:** I was copying it.

**TEACHER:** Why are you late? Doesn't your watch tell time?

**CASSIE:** No, Teacher, you have to look at it.

**TEACHER:** Where do blue eggs
      come from?
**PATSY:** From sad chickens.

**TEACHER:** Why do chickens lay eggs?
**RAMONA:** Because if they dropped them, they
would break.

**TEACHER:** How do they grade chickens?
**LENORE:** They give them eggs-ams.

**VERN:** What do you do for an injured bird?
**FERN:** Give it a first-aid tweetment.

**TEACHER:** Name four members of the cat family.

**FLIP:** Mother, father, sister, and brother.

**TEACHER:** Name six wild animals.

**FLOP:** Two lions and four tigers.

**DOT:** If an African lion fought an African tiger, who would win?

**TEACHER:** Neither. There are no tigers in Africa.

Why weren't the elephants
allowed in the school
swimming pool?
**Because they couldn't keep
their trunks up.**

**TEACHER:** Where are elephants found?
**LOIS:** We don't have to find elephants. They're so
big they don't get lost.

What would happen if an elephant sat in
front of you in class?
**You'd never see the blackboard.**

Why don't many elephants go to college?
**Because so few graduate from high school.**

What is the smartest animal?
**The skunk, because it makes a lot of scents.**

**TEACHER:** How does a skunk defend itself?
**HAZEL:** Instinct.

**SAL:** Where are you taking that skunk?
**VAL:** To school.
**SAL:** What about the smell?
**VAL:** Oh, he'll get used to it.

What was the butterfly's favorite subject?
**Mothematics.**

Who invented fractions?
**Henry the Eighth!**

What kind of food do math teachers eat?
**Square meals.**

Why was the math book unhappy?
**It had too many problems.**

How did the flower do on its exams?
**It got all Bs.**

Why were the little witches up all night?
**They were studying for a hex-amination.**

Why did the little vampires stay up all night?
**They were studying for a blood test.**

**FLIP:** I failed every test
except Spanish.

**FLOP:** How did you keep
from failing that?

**FLIP:** I didn't take Spanish.

**SANDY:** What kind of marks
did you get in gym class?

**MANDY:** I didn't get any marks
— only a skinned knee.

**JOE:** Teacher, I don't think I deserve
a zero on this test.

**TEACHER:** Neither do I, but it's the
lowest mark I can give you.

**TEACHER:** I hope I didn't see you looking at
Don's paper.

**GINGER:** I hope you didn't either.

How is an English teacher like a judge?
**They both hand out sentences.**

In what reference book would you find famous owls?
**"Whoo's Who."**

What would you get if you crossed a book of nursery rhymes and an orange?
**Mother Juice.**

How does a book about zombies begin?
**With a dead-ication.**

## What are the longest words in the English language?

Smiles, because there is a mile between the first and last letters.

Rubber, because it stretches.

Post office, because it has the most letters in it.

Equator, because it circles the globe.

**TEACHER:** If "can't" is short for "cannot," what is "don't" short for?
**SILLY SALLY:** Donut.

**NAN:** Is the food in your school spicy?

**DAN:** No, smoke always comes out of my ears.

What was the computer doing in the school lunchroom?
**Having a byte.**

What is a mushroom?
**Where they store the cafeteria food.**

What is the worst thing you're likely to find in the school cafeteria?
**The food.**

Where do smart hot dogs
end up?
**On the honor roll.**

What happened to the bad
egg in the lunchroom?
**It got egg-spelled.**

What's the difference between a teacher and a donut?
**You can't dunk a teacher in a glass of milk.**

**SUSANNA:** There's a fly in this ice cream.
**CAFETERIA WORKER:** Serves him right.
  Let him freeze.

**MARK:** The crust on this
  apple pie was tough.
**CAFETERIA WORKER:** That
  wasn't the crust. That was
  the paper plate.

**ANNIE:** I thought this was
  supposed to be pea soup,
  but it tastes like soap!
**CAFETERIA WORKER:** Oh,
  it must be tomato soup.
  Pea soup tastes like
  gasoline.

*One of the kids in my class is so mean —*

> he makes the teacher stay after school.
>
> his parents ran away from home.
>
> when he comes to school, the teacher plays hookey.
>
> when he tried to join the human race, he was turned down.

**TEACHER:** How many months have 28 days?
**ROSCOE:** All of them.

**TEACHER:** What is the shortest month?
**LISA:** May. It has only three letters.

**TEACHER:** How many seconds are there in a year?
**HARVEY:** Twelve. January 2nd, February 2nd, March 2nd...

**TEACHER:** What does the Christmas tree stand for?
**TEENA:** It would take up too much room lying down.

**TEACHER:** What nationality is
Santa Claus?
**GARY:** North Polish.

**TEACHER:** What do we
have in December that
we don't have in any
other month?
**VICKIE:** The letter D.

"Will these stairs take me to the principal's office?"
**"No, you have to climb them."**

What would you get if you crossed one principal with another principal?
**Don't do it. Principals don't like to be crossed.**

What animals spend most of the day in the principal's office?
**Cheetahs.**

**PRINCIPAL:** This is the fifth time this week you've been in my office. What do you have to say for yourself?

**JOSEPH:** I'm glad it's Friday.

**PRINCIPAL:** What is your name, young man?

**HENRY:** Henry.

**PRINCIPAL:** Say 'sir.'"

**HENRY:** Okay — Sir Henry!

**PRINCIPAL:** If you study hard, you'll get ahead.

**JANE:** No, thanks. I already have a head.

**TEACHER:** Josh, what can you tell us about the Dead Sea?
**JOSH:** I didn't even know it was sick!

**TEACHER:** What is raised in Brazil during the rainy season?
**ALAN:** Umbrellas.

**TEACHER:** Where is Timbuktu?
**HERBERT:** Between Timbuk-one and Timbuk-three.

**TEACHER:** George, go to the map and find North America.
**GEORGE:** Here it is!
**TEACHER:** Correct. Now, class, who discovered America?
**CLASS:** George!

**TEACHER** *(writing on the blackboard):* I ain't had no fun all summer. Now how should I correct that?

**MIKEY:** Get a hobby.

**SECOND-GRADER:** I really liked being in your class, Mr. Jones. I'm sorry you're not smart enough to teach us next year.

What's the difference between a teacher and a train engineer?
**One trains the mind, the other minds the train.**

What's the difference between a train and a teacher?
**One says "Choo-choo," and the other says, "Take the gum out of your mouth."**

**JO:** Where do bugs go in winter?

**MOE:** Search me.

**JO:** No, thanks. I just wondered if you knew.

**TEACHER:** Did you take a bath today?

**KEITH:** Why? Is one missing?

**TEACHER:** Tommy, why do you always get so dirty?

**TOMMY:** Well, I'm a lot closer to the ground than you are.

**TEACHER:** The brain is a wonderful thing.

**DORIS:** Why do you say that?

**TEACHER:** Because it starts working the minute you get up in the morning and never stops until you're called on in class.

Knock-Knock.
   **Who's there?**
Orson.
   **Orson who?**
Orson around gets you kept after school.

What did the insect use to write its book report?
   **Flypaper.**

Why did the lettuce study so hard?
   **It wanted to be at the head of the class.**

What subject do runners like best?

**Jog-raphy.**

What color is a cheerleader?

**Yeller.**

COACH: Good basketball players can jump higher than a fence.

STUDENT: I didn't know fences could jump.

What three R's do cheerleaders learn at school?

**"Rah, rah, rah!"**

Why do soccer players do well in school?

**They use their heads.**

Why did the train go to the gym?

**To join the track team.**

Why did Cinderella flunk out of gym class?

**She had a pumpkin for a coach.**

Why did the little kid bring a glass of water to the basketball game?

**So he could learn how to dribble.**

What do librarians take with them when they go fishing?
**Bookworms.**

Where do sick librarians go to get well?
**To the hush-pital.**

What is the world's tallest building?
**The library. It has the most stories.**

What vegetables do you usually
find in the library?
**Quiet peas.**

Why do elephants have
cracks between their toes?
**For carrying their
library cards.**

What kind of car do
librarians drive?
**Bookmobiles.**

**TEACHER:**  Why did the germ cross the microscope?

**SONYA:**  To get to the other slide.

**TEACHER:**  How fast does light travel?

**MARCEL** (yawning)**:**  I don't know, Teacher, but it gets here too early in the morning.

**TEACHER:**  How do you charge a battery?

**JOANIE:**  With a credit card.

**TEACHER:** What is camphor?

**SYLVIA:** For having fun in the summer.

**TEACHER:** Which is faster — hot or cold?

**STEPHANIE:** Hot. You can always catch cold.

**TEACHER:** What kind of water can't freeze?

**NED:** Hot water.

What is the difference between a dressmaker and the school nurse?

**One cuts the dresses and the other dresses the cuts.**

**SCHOOL NURSE:** Can I take your pulse?
**BILLY:** Why? Haven't you got one of your own?

**SCHOOL NURSE:** It's well known that exercise kills germs.
**CLASS CLOWN:** Yes, but how do you get the germs to exercise?

**EMMA:** What's the best thing to do for insect bites?
**SCHOOL NURSE:** Don't bite any.

**MOTHER:** What did you learn in school today?

**AUDREY:** Not enough. I have to go again tomorrow.

**FATHER:** What did you learn in school today?

**LOUIE:** My teacher taught us how to write.

**FATHER:** What did you write?

**LOUIE:** I don't know, Dad. She didn't teach us how to read yet.

**FATHER:** What did you learn in school today?

**SON:** I learned to say "Yes, sir," "No, sir," and "Thank you."

**FATHER:** You did?

**SON:** Yup.

**MOTHER:** Do you like going to school?

**SON:** Yes, and I like to come home, too. It's the time in between that I don't like.

**TEACHER:** At your age, I could name all the presidents and in the right order.

**PETER:** Well, sure — but at that time there were probably only five of them.

**TEACHER:** Where was the Declaration of Independence signed?

**MICKEY:** At the bottom.

**TEACHER:** When crossing the Delaware River, why did George Washington stand up in the boat?

**CLASS CLOWN:** He was afraid if he sat down someone would hand him an oar.

**FATHER:** I hear you played hookey from school to play baseball.

**JUNIOR:** I did not play baseball! I have the fish to prove it!

**VOICE** (on telephone): My son has a bad cold and won't be able to attend school today.

**ASSISTANT PRINCIPAL:** Who is this?

**VOICE:** This is my father speaking.

Why was the scissors thrown out of school?
**It kept cutting classes.**

**Knock-Knock.**
Who's there?
**Alice.**
Alice who?
**Alice thinking is giving
me a headache.**

**FRANK:** Day after day, the boy and
his dog went to school together.
Then the day came when they
had to part.
**HANK:** What happened?
**FRANK:** The dog graduated.

"Emily," said the teacher, "I don't know what I'm
going to do with you. Everything goes in one ear
and out the other."
**"Of course," said Emily, "isn't that why we have
two ears?"**

What letter comes after A?
**All of them.**

What comes after B?
**Quiet.**

What comes after G?
**Whiz.**

What comes after O?
**Yeah.**

How does the alphabet say goodbye?
**"A B C'ing you!"**

# INDEX